Pride and Prejudice

A Graphic Revision Guide for GCSE English Literature

Elizabeth May

Brilliant
PUBLICATIONS

We hope you and your pupils enjoy using the ideas in this book. Brilliant Publications publishes many other books to help teachers. To find out more details on any of the titles listed below, please go to our website: **www.brilliantpublications.co.uk**.

By the same author
The Strange Case of Dr Jekyll and Mr Hyde: A Graphic Revision Guide for GCSE English Literature
Jane Eyre: A Graphic Revision Guide for GCSE English Literature

Other literacy titles

How to Dazzle at Macbeth	978-1-897675-93-9
How to Dazzle at Romeo and Juliet	978-1-897675-92-2
How to Dazzle at Twelfth Night	978-1-903853-34-4
How to Dazzle at Reading	978-1-897675-44-1
How to Dazzle at Reading for Meaning	978-1-897575-51-9
How to Dazzle at Writing	978-1-897675-45-8
How to Dazzle at Spelling	978-1-897675-47-2
How to Dazzle at Grammar	978-1-897675-46-5

Published by Brilliant Publications Limited
Unit 10
Sparrow Hall Farm
Edlesborough
Dunstable
Bedfordshire
LU6 2ES, UK

www.brilliantpublications.co.uk

The name Brilliant Publications and the logo are registered trademarks.

Written and illustrated by Elizabeth May
Cover illustrated by Elizabeth May
Cover design by Brilliant Publications Limited

© Text and illustrations Elizabeth May 2018
© Design Brilliant Publications Limited 2018

Printed ISBN 978-0-85747-687-6
ePDF ISBN   978-0-85747-694-4
First printed and published in the UK in 2018
10 9 8 7 6 5 4 3 2 1

Contents

Introduction

In GCSE Literature there are long and complicated plots to follow and concepts to grasp that can be overwhelming for any student. For SEN students in particular, the importance of visuals to aid learning can never be underestimated. 65 per cent of us are visual learners, and all of us can benefit from having large amounts of complex information repackaged in a fun, engaging and simple way.

This book contains photocopiable resources that will strengthen students' understanding of *Pride and Prejudice* in a format that is easily accessible and highly visual. It is ideal for students who want to support their study of this landmark novel, and teachers who want to support their lessons.

In this book, you will find the story of *Pride and Prejudice* re-told in comic form, guide pages to aspects of the story, illustrations and activity pages. These will all strengthen the student's understanding of plot, characters, quotes, themes and much more.

How will this book be effective?

Exam specifications

The major exam boards (AQA, Edexcel and OCR) all look for very similar things when judging a student's performance. Here are the key skills a student should demonstrate to score highly; alongside are the pages in the book most relevant to that skill:

Skill	pages
Understand and analyse words, phrases and sentences in context.	47–50, 60–66, 71–72
Explore plot, characterisation, settings and events.	7–46, 51–59, 67–68, 73
Talk about different themes.	60–66
Generate opinions on the text.	74–76, 79–81
Support their point of view using quotes and knowledge about context.	47–55, 61–66, 71–73, 77
Show how language, form and structure of the text shapes its meaning.	7–50, 71–72

SEN

These resources are suitable for any level of study, but are specifically tailored to GCSE study. They are tailored to be accessible to students with special educational needs (SEN). To do this, the book uses the following criteria:

∗ A heavy focus on visuals: using visual aids to learn is an educational recommendation for most SEN students. It helps students to remember, understand, get interested in, and create associations to the text.

∗ A focus on plot comprehension: one of the biggest unaddressed stumbling blocks for SEN students. Chapter summaries are condensed to include key events, and are image-based to help students remember what happened and consolidate a full picture of the plot.

∗ Simple language for greater accessibility.

∗ A focus on vocabulary: explaining and rephrasing tricky words.

∗ A focus on key quotes that all students are more likely to be able to comprehend and remember more easily.

Although this book has been created to be accessible for SEN students generally, here is how it can benefit some different types of SEN specifically:

∗ Provides a large amount of visual aids (LDD, ASD, SLCN, PNI, ADD, Dyslexia).

∗ Uses clear language (ASD, SLCN). – Uses vocabulary lists and aims to develop vocabulary (LDD, ASD, SLCN).

* Breaks things down into small steps – particularly plot (LDD, ASD, ADD).

* Uses a range of activities (LDD, ADD). – Encourages forming an opinion on, and empathising with, characters (ASD, SLCN).

* Repeats specific images and quotes (SLCN, ASD, Dyslexia).

Key:

ADD – Attention Deficit Disorder

ASD – Autistic Spectrum Disorder

LDD – Learning Difficulties and Disabilities

PNI – Physical and Neurological Impairments

SLCN – Speech, Language and Communication Needs

Part One

New Neighbours

1 One day, in a house called Longbourn in Hertfordshire, England, a lady called Mrs Bennet hears there is a new man in town.

Mr Bennet! Did you hear?

Hm?

A rich single man called Mr Bingley has moved into Netherfield!

Mrs Bennet

Mr Bennet

So?

So if you go and visit him, maybe he can meet our daughters ...

... and end up marrying one of them!

Hmm .... nah.

GAAAH

WHY NOT?

HEH HEH HEH

The five daughters in the Bennet family hear the news.

Mary

Lydia

Jane

Elizabeth

Kitty

2

I can't believe your father won't visit Mr Bingley.

Elizabeth

Mama, there will be a ball in two weeks – we can just meet him there.

Mr Bennet thinks his wife's worrying is quite funny and makes some silly suggestions about how to meet Mr Bingley …

Oh, Mr Bennet!

… but then he announces:

WHAT?!

Actually, I visited Bingley this morning. So we should meet him soon.

3 Bingley comes to Longbourn for a quick chat with Mr Bennet.

Charles Bingley

Thank you for inviting me to your lovely home! I look forward to meeting your family at the next ball!

2 weeks later …

The Bennet ladies go to the ball. They spot Bingley and see that he has a very handsome friend.

Soon however, everyone notices Bingley's friend is being quite grumpy and rude.

Elizabeth doesn't really like Bingley's sisters either.

Fitzwilliam Darcy

Wow! WHO'S HE? CUTE!

Come on Darcy. Dance! Socialise!

No.

What a proud man!

Louisa Caroline

However, everyone is quite pleased with Bingley, who is kind and polite …

Later, Elizabeth hears her name mentioned.

Jane

… and likes Elizabeth's sister Jane a lot.

Why don't you dance with Elizabeth?

She's not pretty enough for me. You are dancing with the only pretty girl here.

Hah!

4 Jane and Elizabeth talk about the ball.

Oh, Lizzy! Bingley was such a fine gentleman!

His sisters were lovely too!

Yes, Bingley was great! I'm pleased he likes you!

What, Caroline and Louisa? No, I didn't like them at all.

5 The Bennet girls are friends with the Lucas family who live at Lucas Lodge.

The families meet to gossip about the ball.

Lady Lucas

Sir William Lucas

Charlotte Lucas

Hello, dear Charlotte!

Seems like Bingley really liked Jane! I heard him say Jane was the prettiest girl at the ball!

Oh, I hope so!

Yep, he loves my Jane!

But poor Lizzy! Darcy said you weren't pretty! How rude!

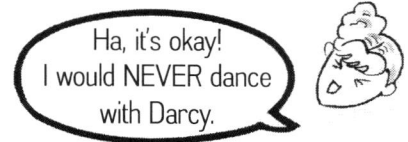

Ha, it's okay! I would NEVER dance with Darcy.

6 After the ball, Louisa and Caroline decide they'd like to get to know Jane and Elizabeth better.

Jane and Bingley also get closer.

Hmm ....

Well, I suppose Jane and Bingley will marry! Everyone is thinking it!

Is it just me who finds that a bit silly?

They've known each other for two weeks!

Well, we both know marriage isn't about love.

SIGH

Yes. It's all about money. And entails.

Over at Netherfield ...

hmm...

Darcy has been thinking about Elizabeth, even though he said before that she wasn't pretty.

Later, at Lucas Lodge ...

Sir William Lucas throws a ball.

Elizabeth notices that Darcy is watching her.

He reluctantly asks her to dance.

No thank you.

He tells Caroline about his crush.

Elizabeth has nice eyes.

What? HER?

7 In a nearby town, Meryton, a militia have come to stay.

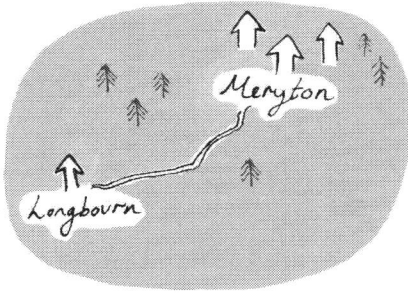

Kitty and Lydia are excited.

Hearing about Jane's invitation to Netherfield, Mrs Bennet has a plan.

Elizabeth walks all the way to Netherfield.

---

8 | That evening ...

While Elizabeth is looking after her, the others gossip about her.

Jane is still unwell.

So, didn't it put you off Elizabeth, seeing her all muddy and sweaty?

No. She was still pretty.

Grrr ...

Elizabeth comes down, and they all talk about what it means to be an 'accomplished' woman – Darcy and Elizabeth disagree.

I don't know many ladies that are actually accomplished.

Well, your standards are too high!

Later ...

Jane still isn't better so Elizabeth stays the night at Netherfield.

9 | Mrs Bennet, Lydia and Kitty arrive at Netherfield to see Jane.

The Bennets chat with the Bingleys.

A doctor comes to look at her too.

Please don't be embarrassing ...

Please throw a ball here, Mr Bingley!

Is she okay?

She's fine. She just needs some rest.

I would love to!

I'm glad you enjoy being here in the country, Mr Bingley!

10 The next day …

Downstairs, Darcy is trying to write a letter to his younger sister, Georgiana, but Caroline keeps distracting him.

Jane is still recovering.

You write so quickly. How's that pen? Shall I mend it for you?

When he is finished, he and Elizabeth find another thing to disagree about: "changing your opinion".

You should never change your opinions to please someone else.

Why not? Isn't it a good thing to be able to change your mind and listen to your friends?

Please stop arguing!

Later …

Shall we dance?

No!

HEH HEH

Caroline is jealous that Darcy likes Elizabeth.

What can Charles and Darcy like about the Bennets?! They don't have much money, and the mother is so annoying!

Caroline and Louisa are rude to Elizabeth when they bump into her in the garden.

There's not enough room on this path for all of us.

I can't wait to go home.

11 Jane is feeling better, and goes downstairs with Elizabeth.

Caroline is only interested in Darcy ... and keeps trying to distract him.

Elizabeth, let's walk around the room together.

Umm ... okay.

I know you just want my attention.

Elizabeth and Darcy get into yet another small argument.

Well, that's rude!

He's just being ridiculous. Let's laugh at him.

I might be ridiculous, but at least I don't misunderstand people on purpose!

At least I don't hate everyone!

12

Elizabeth and Jane finally go home.

What? They're back already? They should have stayed longer!

Darcy is happy that Elizabeth has gone so he doesn't have to keep seeing her and be bothered by his attraction to her.

Now I can relax.

Elizabeth and Jane are happy to be home again. Kitty and Lydia tell them all about the soldiers in Meryton.

Some of the officers dined with our uncle!

And Colonel Forster might get married!

Mr Collins Visits

13

Bad news, everyone! My annoying relative, Mr Collins, is coming to stay.

Mr Collins

Dear Mr Bennet,
I am coming over! We need to make peace, since you and my father had that big argument. Also, the wonderful Lady Catherine de Bourgh suggested I should come.
Mr Collins

Mr Collins arrives, and everyone thinks he is annoying.

Mr Collins will inherit Longbourn when Mr Bennet dies. That means he is checking out his future house. He is also determined to make one of the Bennet girls his wife.

KNOCK KNOCK

Hello, dear Bennets!

Did I tell you about my neighbour, Lady Catherine de Bourgh?

Yes, hello ...

No thanks.

Ugh!

I just want Bingley.

14 Mr Collins continues to annoy the Bennets.

Her Ladyship lives in Rosings Park, a beautiful mansion right next to my house!

Her daughter is the most charming young lady.

I always compliment her. Ladies love my compliments.

If you say so ...

15

Later …

Mr Collins tags along to Meryton with the Bennet girls.

When they arrive …

The girls go over to the two men.

The Bennets (and Mr Collins) chat to Denny and Wickham for a while, and then …

… Darcy and Bingley arrive!

The Bennets go to their aunt's house in Meryton.

I like the officers too! So handsome!

I'll invite that Wickham to dine here – and you girls too!

Mrs Phillips

Hooray!

Splendid! I'll come too.

Jane, did you notice how awkward it was between the men earlier?

Yes – I wonder why?

16 | At the Phillips' dinner party ...

Wickham has a lot to say about Darcy.

Elizabeth gets talking to Wickham. She decides she likes him.

Darcy is such a disagreeable man!

He is!

I think you should know – he is a very bad man! He treated me scandalously!

His father liked me and so was going to leave me the church he owned after he died, so I could have my dream job – a clergyman. But after he died, Darcy stopped me from getting the church because he hates me!

Oh my! How awful of him!

17 Elizabeth tells Jane about what Wickham said.

Later …

Bingley, Caroline and Louisa have an invitation for the Bennets.

Elizabeth is in such a good mood that she willingly talks to Mr Collins.

18 It's the Netherfield ball!

Elizabeth looks for Wickham, but he doesn't show up.

Oh, Charlotte! I'm so disappointed. Where is Wickham?

Excuse me, but I believe we ought to dance!

Ah ... yes.

Later ...

Darcy asks Elizabeth to dance.

Miss Bennet, dance with me.

Huh? What? Yes, okay!

Oh, why did I say yes?

They dance – but Darcy is quiet.

Elizabeth brings up Wickham.

So ... seems like Wickham doesn't like you much.

Don't judge me before you know me.

Darcy walks off angry ...

... but he doesn't stay angry for long since he really likes Elizabeth.

Elizabeth, I heard you talking about Wickham. Don't believe him. He is the one who treated Darcy badly.

Caroline approaches Elizabeth.

Hmm, I don't think so, Caroline.

Jane, has Bingley said anything about Wickham?

Not really, no.

Elizabeth spends the rest of the ball feeling quite embarrassed by her family ...

... Mr Collins tries desperately to speak to Darcy after finding out he is Lady Catherine's nephew ...

... Mrs Bennet keeps voicing her opinions loudly ...

... and Mary plays the piano badly.

20

You said no?!

Yes. Why would I want to marry him?

Oh! Did you not think of the money? The house?

Charlotte comes along.

Well, I think she made the right decision. He's awful.

Oh Mr Bennet!

You won't believe what's happened!

Uh ...

Charlotte! Lizzy REJECTED Mr Collins! Don't you think that's awful?

If none of you girls get married we will end up on the street!!

It's okay. I changed my mind.

Oh, Elizabeth!

21 Mr Collins tries to avoid Elizabeth.

Later, the Bennet girls go to Meryton again, and they find Wickham.

Mr Wickham, I looked for you at the ball!

Oh yes. I didn't want to go, since Darcy was there.

Later ...

KNOCK KNOCK
Letter for Jane!

Dear Jane, We have all left Netherfield and we won't be back for a long time. We will be in London ...

Oh no!

We will be spending time with Darcy's sister, Georgiana. I think Charles might end up wanting to marry her! That would be good, wouldn't it? - Caroline

Jane, don't worry! This is just Caroline's side of the story.

22 Mr Collins has proposed to Charlotte Lucas. (Elizabeth's close friend).

Then, Mr Collins goes home.

Elizabeth has an outburst.

WHAT?

What are you thinking Charlotte?!

Don't judge me, Lizzy. Not everyone hates Mr Collins like you do.

23 Sir William comes over to officially announce Charlotte's engagement.

Charlotte is going to marry Mr Collins!

But he asked Lizzy to marry him!

It's true. He then proposed to Charlotte.

I'll never forgive you for saying no to him, Lizzy!

Sir William and Lady Lucas are very happy.

However, things have become a bit awkward between Charlotte and Elizabeth.

Mr Collins sends a letter to the Bennets, saying …

Thank you so much for letting me stay with you. I will come back again very soon, so I can see my lovely Charlotte again.
– Mr. Collins

GROAN

Again?

Elizabeth and Jane still haven't heard anything from Bingley.

What if Charles never comes back?

Oh dear …

Later …

Yoohoo!

Mr Collins comes back to the Bennets' house again.

Part Two

24 A letter comes from Caroline.

KNOCK KNOCK

Letter for Jane!

We'll be in London for a long time still. We are all enjoying lovely Georgiana's company. Charles really likes her!
~ Caroline

Oh dear ...

Jane, think about it! It doesn't make any sense. Bingley liked you. It must have been Caroline and Darcy who made him move away.

So no husband for Jane, either?!

Maybe you can find a man to disappoint you too, Lizzy!

Now that Darcy is out of town, Wickham tells everyone the story about him.

... and then he stopped me from getting my dream job!

25 It's Christmas!

Mr Collins has been spending a lot of time with Charlotte.

Then he goes home.

New visitors come from Longbourn: Mrs Bennet's brother and his wife.

Mrs Gardiner

Mr Gardiner

Mrs Gardiner consoles Jane about Bingley moving away.

Jane, I know you are sad. Come to London with me and your uncle when we leave. It might cheer you up.

26 Mrs Gardiner has some advice for Elizabeth.

Jane leaves with the Gardiners to go to London.

Elizabeth, I heard that you like Wickham these days. I think that you should not fall in love with him.

Hmm, you're probably right. He isn't rich, after all.

A letter comes from Charlotte telling Elizabeth about life in Hunsford with Mr Collins.

Then, a letter comes from Jane.

KNOCK KNOCK

Letter for Elizabeth!

It's going okay. Please come and visit me soon! ~ Charlotte

You were right about Caroline! I went to visit her...

Oh, hello ...

... but she obviously was not interested in being friends anymore.

Elizabeth is starting to notice that Wickham isn't talking to her as much now, as he has met a rich young lady, Miss King.

She doesn't really mind, though.

Miss King

Oh, well. I don't care. This must mean I don't have feelings for him.

Hunsford and Rosings

27

A few months pass and it's March.

Mrs Gardiner has heard about Wickham's interest in Miss King.

On the way there, she stops in London to see Jane.

Elizabeth leaves Longbourn to visit Charlotte and Mr Collins. Charlotte's father and sister come too.

It is rather disappointing, yes ...

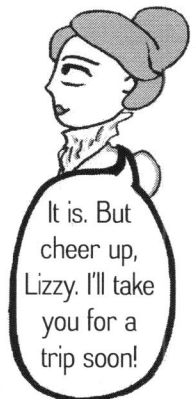

It is. But cheer up, Lizzy. I'll take you for a trip soon!

28

Elizabeth and Charlotte's father and sister arrive at the Collins' house in Hunsford, Kent.

Mr Collins is being annoying as usual, but Elizabeth can see that Charlotte is fairly happy.

I can do nice things all day while he's in the garden!

Blah blah... look at our beautiful curtains... blah blah blah ...

Maria Lucas

Later ...

Elizabeth, come look at this! Quick!

... so we will see you all there soon.

Everyone has been invited to dine at **Rosings**, Lady Catherine de Bourgh's house!

Anne de Bourgh

Mrs Jenkinson

29 Everyone is excited about dining at Rosings …

… except Elizabeth.

What's the big deal? It's just rich people …

After a very short walk, the group arrive at Rosings.

At dinner, the conversation is quite awkward.

Lady Catherine de Bourgh

Such an excellent dinner, your Ladyship!

Later …

Lady Catherine asks Elizabeth lots of questions about her upbringing.

So how old are you? Did you have a governess when you were a child?

30

Sir William Lucas leaves Hunsford after a week, which means Mr Collins stops showing off so much.

A few weeks later …

Darcy turns up in Hunsford to visit his relatives with a friend. Mr Collins brings them back to the house.

Colonel Fitzwilliam

Darcy goes up to Elizabeth.

So how are you?

I'm okay …

I could find out what's going on with Bingley …

Did you know that Jane has been in London recently? Have you seen her?

No …

31

Everyone is at Rosings.

Miss Bennet, why don't you play the piano for us?

Okay ...

Darcy, stop staring at me please.

Quite annoyed at Darcy, Elizabeth tells Colonel Fitzwilliam about his behaviour in Hertfordshire.

... he didn't dance with or speak to anyone!

I'm not good at talking to strangers.

32

Darcy comes to the Collins' parsonage, but is surprised to find only Elizabeth there.

Hello!

They chat awkwardly.

So how's Bingley?

He is fine.

Later ...

I wonder why Darcy stayed so long to talk awkwardly instead of just leaving?

I suppose he was just bored.

Darcy keeps doing things like this.

Hello again ...

Elizabeth starts to consider whether Colonel Fitzwilliam would make a good husband for her.

He does like me ... could I marry him?

No, I don't love him.

Elizabeth's Opinion Changes

34 Darcy bursts into the parsonage.

He walks up and down, and then says …

Miss Bennet, I must tell you how much I love you!

But I'm not happy about it as you are not really rich and classy enough for me.

WHAT?!

But it's okay. Marry me.

Mr Darcy, I would NEVER marry you! You are so rude! AND you split up Jane and Bingley! AND you were awful to Wickham! So NO!

!!!!

Darcy leaves quickly.

35 Darcy waits around to give a letter to Elizabeth.

Elizabeth reads the letter. It is shocking.

Dear Miss Bennet, You are right, I did try to stop Bingley from marrying Jane. I don't regret it. I believe she didn't truly love him.

I also thought that Bingley should not marry into your family, as he is more rich and important and civilised. Sorry.

As for Wickham… he is a liar! I gave him the money my father left for him, but he didn't want to be a clergyman, he wanted to study law. He said he would give up the church…

…in exchange for £3000! So I gave him the £3000, and he spent it all. **Then** he wanted the church. I refused. So, he wanted to punish me. He ran off with my sister, Georgiana, and tried to marry her.

I believe he was after my sister's money. Luckily I stopped them in time, though. So this is what Wickham is really like. I hope you believe me. ~ Darcy

36 Elizabeth keeps thinking about and re-reading Darcy's letter.

She remembers things about Wickham ...

... like him not coming to the ball ...

... and becoming interested in the recently rich Miss King.

She can also see Darcy's point about Jane – their family had not acted in a sophisticated, reputable way in front of Darcy.

It all makes sense!

37 Elizabeth is constantly thinking about the letter.

She gets angry at herself.

He's right about my family!

I acted so badly towards Darcy!

If that's true about Wickham ...

Later ...

I will be going home. My father misses me.

So soon?

Lizzie, come back!

38 Elizabeth and Maria leave Hunsford.

They go to London for a few days with Jane and the Gardiners.

Elizabeth wonders whether she should tell Jane about Darcy's letter.

39

Jane, Elizabeth and Maria go back to Hertfordshire. On the way to meet Mr Bennet's carriage, they meet Kitty and Lydia.

They dine together and Lydia gossips.

Wickham can't go after Miss King anymore! She's gone to Liverpool!

Later they arrive at Longbourn.

40 Elizabeth finally tells Jane about Darcy's proposal and about Wickham.

... And then he went off with Georgiana!

(She doesn't mention what Darcy wrote about her and Bingley.)

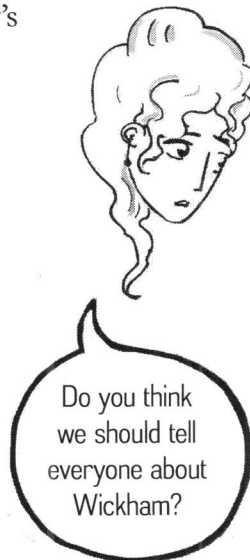

Do you think we should tell everyone about Wickham?

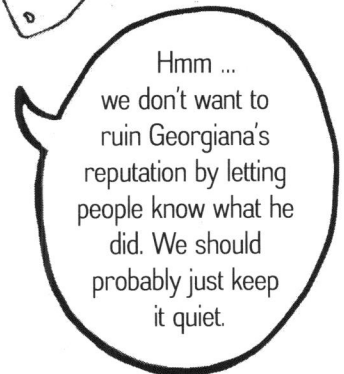

Hmm ... we don't want to ruin Georgiana's reputation by letting people know what he did. We should probably just keep it quiet.

41 The militia are going to leave Meryton.

Lydia gets an invitation from Colonel Forster's wife.

Dear Lydia,
We are going to Brighton with the militia. We would like to invite you along with us!
~ Mrs Forster

KNOCK KNOCK

Letter for Lydia!

Hmph!

What about me?

Oh, fantastic! I'm going to Brighton with the officers!

Here she goes again ... she will disgrace the Bennet family in Brighton ...

Oh, it's okay Lizzy. How could Lydia's behaviour affect **your** reputation?

If you let Lydia go to Brighton she will embarrass us all with her behaviour!

Ugh!

Later, at a gathering ...

Elizabeth sees Wickham and wants to subtly let him know she found out about his lies.

I've been spending a lot of time with Darcy.

Oh?

Lydia leaves for Brighton with the Forsters.

My opinion of him has improved.

I see ...

42 Still thinking about Darcy's letter, and about her conversation with Mr Bennet.

I don't think my father really tried hard to bring us up well.

And I don't think my parents are a well-suited couple either.

Later on ...

The Bennet's receive letters from Lydia in Brighton.

*Dear everyone,
I'm having such a wonderful time!!! I'm buying lots of lovely things and meeting lots of handsome men!
~ Lydia xxx*

Elizabeth is looking forward to going on the trip to the lakes that Mrs Gardiner promised.

However, there is a change of plan.

Lizzy, it turns out we can't go to the lakes!

Yes, I am needed at work. We will just have to go to Derbyshire instead.

Oh, that's okay.

Do you know what? We should visit Pemberley – Darcy's mansion – when we go to Derbyshire.

Um... as long as he won't be there when we go!

Oh, he won't be!

Part Three

Lambton and Pemberley

43 Elizabeth, Mr and Mrs Gardiner arrive in Pemberley, which is beautiful.

They are given a tour of the house by the housekeeper, who keeps telling them how wonderful and kind Darcy is.

Darcy is the best master I could ask for!

Mrs Reynolds

Gosh, he sounds like a really good person.

They all go out to the gardens.

Suddenly … Darcy appears.

He talks to everyone. Elizabeth feels embarrassed and uncomfortable.

It's good to see you …

He leaves, and Elizabeth and the Gardiners continue their walk around the garden.

Darcy approaches them again. He's being very nice.

When the Gardiners and Elizabeth leave, the Gardiners keep saying how impressed they were with Darcy.

Why is he here?!

Mr Gardiner, you are welcome to go fishing on my grounds here!

Miss Bennet, would you like to come and meet the Bingleys tomorrow? And my sister Georgiana?

Lizzy, I thought you said he wasn't nice? He was lovely!

He is perfectly well behaved and polite!

They are right … he really is nice.

44

In Lambton, Derbyshire …

Darcy and Georgiana come to visit Elizabeth and the Gardiners.

Nice to meet you, Georgiana!

Aw, she's so shy!

Bingley comes along too, and is very nice and friendly. Elizabeth watches him to see if he acts interested in Georgiana romantically, like Caroline suggested he was.

He doesn't seem to act at all like he's in love with Georgiana …

They all have a nice time talking and catching up.

Let's all have dinner at Pemberley the night after next!

Before Bingley leaves, he asks Elizabeth how her family is, and says there are things he needs to talk about.

Later …

Elizabeth keeps thinking about Darcy.

45

Elizabeth and the Gardiners are invited to Pemberley.

At Pemberley, they meet Caroline and Louisa, along with Bingley, Darcy, Georgiana, and Mrs Annesley, a woman who lives with Georgiana.

Mrs Annesley

Caroline and Louisa are rude and do not talk to Elizabeth or the Gardiners.

Later …

Caroline starts angrily ranting about Elizabeth.

Miss Bennet looks **bad** today. But I always thought she was quite **ugly**. Don't you agree, Georgiana?

…

Actually, Miss Bennet is one of the most beautiful women I've ever known!

46 Elizabeth gets two letters in the post from Jane.

KNOCK KNOCK

Letters for Elizabeth!

The first one was written five days ago.

Dear Lizzy,
Something very unexpected has happened. Last night we got a very surprising letter from Colonel Forster.

It said that Lydia had run off with Wickham! They have probably gone to Scotland where they can get married easily!
~ Jane

Before Elizabeth can even think about it, she opens the next letter.

It's even worse than she thought.

Dear Lizzy,
Oh, how terrible! It turns out that Wickham does **not** want to marry Lydia, as Colonel Forster found out...

... But they can't live together without marrying!!! Colonel Forster is now out trying to find them in London somewhere. Father will go to help search too. Oh, how dreadful!
~ Jane

Elizabeth starts panicking.

This is AWFUL!

Just then, Darcy walks in.

Miss Bennet! What's wrong? Can I help you?

Elizabeth tells him what the letter said.

... And he is not even going to marry her!

...

Darcy is flustered.

That is really awful. Your poor family! I am sure this means you have to go now. I promise I won't tell anyone.

Soon after ...

Elizabeth and the Gardiners head to Longbourn.

Searching for Lydia

47

In the carriage …

He's got to marry her!

Surely!

Elizabeth feels guilty.

Oh, why didn't I warn everyone about Wickham?

At Longbourn …

Nobody has heard any news. Mrs Bennet is panicking.

Oh, what to do? It's a nightmare!

Mr Gardiner says he will go to London to help Colonel Forster and Mr Bennet find Lydia and Wickham tomorrow.

48

A few days later …

Mr Collins also sends a letter after hearing about what happened.

Mr Gardiner sends a letter to Longbourn.

Dear Bennets,
We are still looking for them – no luck yet.
~ Mr Gardiner

Dear Bennets,
This is a terrible situation. I have told everyone about it. I'm so glad I didn't marry Elizabeth because then I would be disgraced too.

My suggestion is that you never talk to Lydia ever again. I hope you take my advice.
~ Mr Collins

…

Later …

Another letter from Mr Gardiner arrives.

Dear Bennets,
We've been trying to find out if Wickham has any relatives he could be staying with, but it seems like he doesn't have any.

We did find out that Wickham has **huge gambling debts** that he needs to pay in Brighton. That's not good!
~ Mr Gardiner

Mr Bennet comes home to rest from searching.

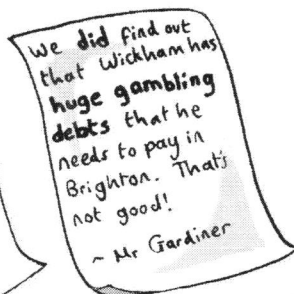

Lizzy, you were right about Lydia before. I think this whole situation might partly be my fault.

49 | 2 days later …

Another letter from Mr Gardiner arrives.

*Dear Bennets, We have found them! They are not married, but Wickham says he **will** marry Lydia if I pay him.*

He wants a lot of money. £10,000. I will pay it for the good of our family's reputation. It has to be done. ~ Mr Gardiner

Well, this is delightful! Lydia will be married! Hooray!

…

…

50 | We learn that Mr Bennet never saved any money because he thought he would have a son, who would inherit his estate.

It's a boy!

Younger Mr Bennet

Mr Bennet is very angry about the situation.

Lydia and Wickham will never be allowed inside this house!

Let them come in when they are married, father!

Ugh, fine.

Elizabeth starts thinking about how perfect Darcy could have been for her.

I think I could have been happy with him …

But now he knows about what Lydia did, he will never want to associate with me or my family again.

Dear Mr Bennet,

Wickham has been paid – let us never mention this again.

Wickham has thankfully moved to a different part of the military, far away from Hertfordshire, in the North. He and Lydia will be nowhere near any of us soon.

~ Mr Gardiner

51 Lydia and Wickham get married.

They come to Longbourn afterwards.

Lydia is loud and excited about being married.

We had such a great time!

Who'd have thought I'd be married before coming back to Longbourn!?

Elizabeth can tell Wickham doesn't like Lydia as much as she likes him.

...

Lydia keeps on talking, and accidentally reveals that Darcy was at her wedding.

... then maybe Darcy wouldn't have shown up!

What?! Darcy was at your wedding?

Oops! My George didn't hear that, did he? It was supposed to be a secret!

What? Why would Darcy have been at the wedding?

Elizabeth writes a letter to Mrs Gardiner to find out what's going on.

Dear Aunt, Lydia has just blurted out that Darcy was at her wedding.

Please can you tell me why he was there? ~ Elizabeth

Getting to know Darcy

52 Mrs Gardiner writes back to Elizabeth.

Dear Lizzy, Honestly, Darcy was at Wickham and Lydia's wedding because he was the one who paid Wickham.

Darcy was also the one who found Wickham and Lydia in London. He tried to make Lydia run away from Wickham but she wouldn't, as she thought they would marry anyway.

Wow! That is so nice of Darcy to go to all that trouble, especially as he hates Wickham.

Could he have done all that for ... me?

Nah ... of course not.

Later ...

Wickham joins Elizabeth on a walk, and wants to know how much she knows about his past.

I know enough about you, believe me, Mr Wickham. Let's just leave it there.

53 The Bennets hear news that Bingley will soon come back to Netherfield.

A few days later ...

Bingley and Darcy arrive at Longbourn. Elizabeth does not dare to look at Darcy.

Oh, I really don't care ...

Yes she does!

Well hello!

Mrs Bennet invites Bingley and Darcy for dinner in a few days time.

54 Elizabeth is confused about why Darcy came along with Bingley to Longbourn but didn't say anything.

I don't get it! Does he want to speak with me or not?

Later ...

Darcy and Bingley come to dine at Longbourn.

Bingley sits by Jane.

Elizabeth hopes to speak to Darcy, but she doesn't get to.

55 Bingley proposes to Jane.

Everyone is happy for Jane and Bingley (especially Mrs Bennet).

Elizabeth jokes that she could never be as lucky as Jane.

... I could only hope for another Mr Collins to come along!

56 Lady Catherine makes a surprise visit to Longbourn.

I need to speak to Elizabeth, alone!

Now listen here, Miss Bennet. You must never even think about marrying Darcy. He's supposed to marry my daughter Anne!

What? Darcy hasn't made another proposal to me ...

Well look ... I'm going to do whatever I want.

WHAT? Are you saying NO to ME?

Lady Catherine leaves in a huff.

57 Elizabeth feels uneasy about the Lady Catherine situation.

Why would she have come here to tell me not to marry Darcy?

KNOCK KNOCK

Letter for Mr. Bennet!

Dear Mr. Bennet,
First of all, congratulations on Jane's marriage. More importantly, though, please know that Elizabeth must NOT marry Darcy. This would be a very bad decision.
~ Mr Collins

What ... ?

HA HA HA

Hey Lizzy, come and hear this!

Mr Collins seems to thinks that Darcy is about to propose to you!

He doesn't even like you! How funny!

Heh... heh... . Yes that would be odd, wouldn't it?

58 A few days later ...

Darcy and Elizabeth finally get some private time to talk.

Darcy and Bingley come to Longbourn.

Mr Darcy, I know that you paid Wickham to marry Lydia. Thank you so much for doing that.

... And, I am sorry about how I acted toward you before.

Darcy and Elizabeth walk on, clearing the air and confessing their true feelings.

I am sorry that you found out, Miss Bennet. Your family owes me nothing.

My feelings for you are still the same.

I like you too ...

59 Elizabeth and Darcy get engaged!

Ellizabeth tells Jane about it.

Oh Lizzy, I'm so pleased for you! But are you sure?

100% sure!

Darcy tells Mr Bennet about the engagement.

I have asked for Elizabeth's hand in marriage.

I see.

Mr Bennet talks to Elizabeth about it.

So he really has proposed to you! Are you sure Lizzy? You're not just doing this because he's rich.

No, father, I really do love him.

Then you have my blessing.

Elizabeth tells Mrs Bennet.

THAT IS WONDERFUL!

60 Elizabeth and Darcy talk about their relationship.

I can't pinpoint that moment!

When did you realise you liked me?

I'll have to tell Lady Catherine about the engagement ...

Elizabeth writes to her aunt.

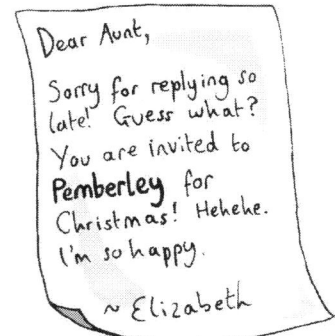

Dear Aunt,
Sorry for replying so late! Guess what? You are invited to **Pemberley** for Christmas! Hehehe. I'm so happy.
~ Elizabeth

Mr Bennet writes a letter to Mr Collins.

Dear Sir,
Elizabeth will be getting married to Darcy. I hope Lady Catherine won't be too upset.

But you know, Darcy is richer than she is, so she might want to be nice about his marriage!
~ Mr Bennet

HEH HEH HEH

This'll show him!

61 Jane and Bingley get married! And Elizabeth and Darcy get married!

The Bennets go to Pemberley often to visit Elizabeth and Darcy (especially Mr Bennet as he misses Elizabeth), and so do the Gardiners, who helped bring the couple together.

Kitty has become more sensible now that she is apart from Lydia. She visits Jane and Elizabeth often.

Mary stays living at Longbourn and begins to socialise more.

Wickham and Lydia ask Darcy and Elizabeth for more money now and then. They give them money, but are not friendly with them.

Lady Catherine remains angry about Darcy marrying Elizabeth for a long time …

But eventually gets over it.

Georgiana moves into Pemberley.

In the end, everyone gets along well, putting the past behind them.

GAAAAH!

Context

Early 19ᵗʰ century England

Time: *Pride and Prejudice* was published in 1813. Jane Austen started writing the book in the 1790s and finished it in the 1810s. The story is set in the early 1800s.

Place: *Pride and Prejudice* is mainly set in Hertfordshire, which is just north of London, in the south of England. Austen uses some made-up place names and some real place names.

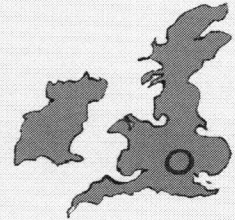

In the early 19th century, England was a place where which class you were in mattered a lot (see Theme: Class page). The middle- and upper-classes did not associate much with the working-classes, which is why *Pride and Prejudice* only has middle- and upper-class characters. Within both of these classes, it was expected that people had to be very polite and hide any negativity they might have felt towards other people. England is at war with France during the story, which is why there are officers like Wickham and Denny around; however, the middle- and upper-classes aren't worried about the war as it doesn't really affect them at all.

Jane Austen

Austen was born in the south of England in 1775. She came from a middle-class family, but in her family were people with lots of money, and people without much at all. Jane was one of the members of the family who did not have a lot of money, because she didn't earn a lot from being a writer. This meant she spent time with people in both the middle- and upper-classes. This part of Jane's life could have influenced the story of *Pride and Prejudice*, wherein a middle-class family with not a lot of money (the Bennets) mixes with upper-class families (the Bingley/Darcy/de Bourgh families).

Austen also had trouble finding a husband. She did want to marry, but in the end she never did. This struggle might have influenced her to write about the problems and complications of love and marriage in *Pride and Prejudice*.

All about ...
Romance Fiction

Stories that focus on a relationship between two lovers can be called 'romance fiction'. Romance novels became popular in the 18th century, the same century that Austen was born in. A lot of people think that Austen influenced this genre as she wrote many popular stories about love and romance. Many people would even say that Austen is one of history's best romance writers.

Romance fiction might include any of the following:

- Following the relationship from its very start

- The couple involved being from different backgrounds/life experiences to each other

- An emphasis on the emotions of the characters

- The couple experiencing 'true love'

- A problem that could stop the relationship

- A happy ending.

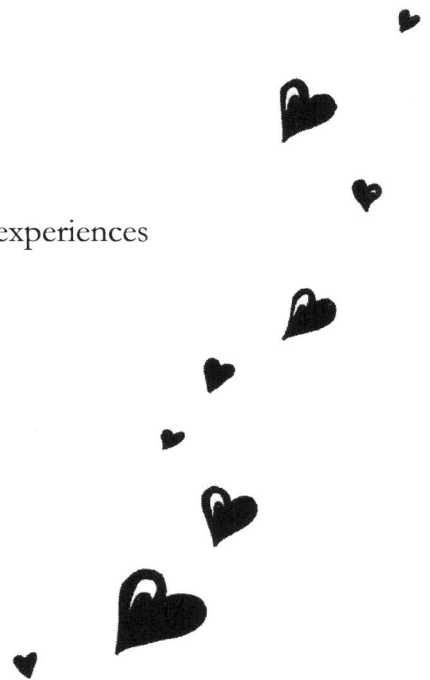

How many of these elements are included in *Pride and Prejudice*?

Why do you think *Pride and Prejudice* has been one of the most widely read and well-loved romance novels of all time?

All about ...
Bildungsroman

A 'bildungsroman' is a genre of novel which follows the main character growing up and learning life lessons. They can also be called 'coming-of-age' stories, as they focus on how a character changes as they get older. Bildungsroman novels might include any of the following:

- The story being narrated in first-person by the main character (the 'protagonist')

- The story beginning in the character's childhood

- The story ending when the main character has achieved happiness

- The main character having trouble fitting in

- The main character facing challenges throughout the story.

Look through each of the above elements of a bildungsroman and think about whether they are true for *Pride and Prejudice*. How much did Elizabeth, the protagonist, change throughout the story? What was it about her that changed? How important is this for the whole story?

Comedy of Manners

The 'comedy of manners' genre **makes fun** of society and social rules, so that they end up looking silly or ridiculous.

In the late 18th and early 19th century, when *Pride and Prejudice* is set, some of the normal things in upper-class society include being polite to everyone, not mixing with the lower-classes, going to assemblies and dinners, marrying for money and marrying quickly.

A comedy of manners novel might include any of the following:

- Upper-class characters

- A society or culture where **money**, **routines** and **politeness** are important

- The society or culture being **made fun of**, or made to look **ridiculous** by the author

- The rules about **manners**, **routines** and **politeness** being broken by a character

- **Stock Characters:** characters who are a **stereotype** of a particular kind of person.

Think about which of the above elements are in *Pride and Prejudice.*
Do you think Jane Austen thought the society and culture of the late 18th century and early 19th century England worked perfectly, or did she think there were some problems?

ELIZABETH

Full name: Elizabeth Bennet

AKA: Lizzy, Eliza, Miss Bennet, Elizabeth Darcy

IMPORTANCE:

100%

> There are few people whom I really love and still fewer of whom I think well.

Fact file:

- Elizabeth is the second eldest of the Bennet sisters at 20

- She is Mr Bennet's favourite daughter. She and Mr Bennet share the same sarcastic sense of humour

- Throughout the story she shows prejudice – judging people before really getting to know them – especially Darcy.

Appearance:
Elizabeth is described as 'pretty' – but not as pretty as Jane. Many people think her eyes are 'so fine'. They are 'dark' and Darcy likes the 'colour' and 'shape' of them.

Caroline thinks Elizabeth's face is 'too thin'.

What people say about her:

BINGLEY

> Very pretty and dare I say very agreeable.
>
> Chapter 3

DARCY

> You taught me a lesson, hard indeed at first, but most advantageous. By you, I was properly humbled.
>
> Chapter 58

> She had a lively, playful disposition, which delighted in anything ridiculous.
>
> chapter 3

AUSTEN (author and narrator)

> Her manners were not of the fashionable world, (but Darcy) was caught by their easy playfulness.
>
> chapter 6

MRS BENNET

> A very headstrong and foolish girl.
>
> Chapter 20

DARCY

IMPORTANCE:

100%

Full name: Fitzwilliam Darcy

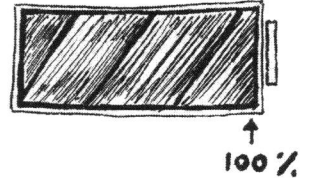

> I was given good principles, but left to follow them in pride and conceit.

Fact file:

- ✪ Darcy is a very rich man in his late twenties

- ✪ He is a close friend of Bingley

- ✪ People think he has a lot of pride, so he is often misunderstood

- ✪ He is very loving and kind – but only to those close to him.

Appearance:
Darcy is 'handsome', 'tall' and 'a fine figure of a man'. The ball-goers in Chapter 3 say he is 'much handsomer than Mr Bingley' – although they say this after finding out how rich he is!

What people say about him:

ELIZABETH

chapter 16

> Very disagreeable

> ill-tempered

chapter 16

> very handsome.

chapter 43

> I hear such different accounts of (Darcy) as puzzle me exceedingly.

chapter 18

MRS REYNOLDS

> He was always the sweetest-tempered, most generous-hearted boy in the world.

chapter 43

chapter 43

> I have never had a cross word from him in all my life, and I have known him since he was four years old.

WICKHAM

chapter 16

> His behaviour to myself has been scandalous.

MRS GARDINER

> Perfectly well-behaved, polite and unassuming.

chapter 43

JANE

Full name: Jane Bennet

AKA: Miss Bennet, the eldest Miss Bennet, Jane Bingley

Fact file:

- At 23, Jane is the eldest of the Bennet sisters

- She is optimistic – she always sees the best in people and tries not to judge anyone

- She is very close to Elizabeth, but sometimes Elizabeth gets annoyed at her for not wanting to say or think anything negative.

> I would not wish to be hasty in censuring anyone.

IMPORTANCE:

70%.

Appearance:
Everyone agrees Jane is good-looking. She is called 'handsome', 'pretty' and 'beautiful'.

What people say about her:

BINGLEY

chapter 3

> The most beautiful creature I ever beheld!

DARCY

chapter 3

> The only handsome girl in the room.

ELIZABETH

> You never see a fault in anybody. All the world are good and agreeable in your eyes.

chapter 4

> You wish to think all the world respectable.

chapter 24

> You are too good.

chapter 24

BINGLEY

Full name: Charles Bingley

70%

Fact file:

- Bingley is a rich young man who starts off the story of *Pride and Prejudice* by renting out Netherfield

- He is polite, kind and happy

- He falls in love with Jane – even though she is not as rich as he is. They marry at the end of the story.

I never met with so many pleasant girls in my life as I have this evening.

Appearance:
Bingley is described by many as 'handsome'. However, the ball goers in Chapter 3, say that he is not as handsome as Darcy. He has a 'pleasant countenance' – a nice face.

What people say about him:

A young man of large fortune from the North of England.
chapter 1

MRS BENNET

So excessively handsome.
chapter 3

Just what a young man ought to be ... sensible, good humoured, lively: and I never saw such happy manners!

So much ease with such perfect good breeding!
chapter 4

JANE

chapter 16
truly amiable

ELIZABETH

Good humour itself
chapter 16

Wickham

Full name: George Wickham

Fact file:

- ⚙ Wickham is a military officer. Before this he tried other jobs

- ⚙ He used to be close to the Darcy family, but he gained a bad reputation when he grew up

- ⚙ He likes to gamble and flirt with women.

IMPORTANCE:

75%

I have been a disappointed man.

Appearance: Wickham has 'beauty', 'fine countenance' (a nice face), and 'a good figure'. Elizabeth thinks his appearance shows he must be a good person ('[your] very countenance may vouch for your being amiable').

ELIZABETH

chapter 47

He has neither integrity nor honour ... he is as false and deceitful as he is inviting.

chapter 26

The most agreeable man I saw.

CAROLINE

George Wickham has treated Mr Darcy in a most infamous manner.

Chapter 18

chapter 25

DARCY

A very proud, ill-natured boy.

chapter 18

Mr Wickham is blessed with such happy manners as may ensure his making friends – whether he may be equally capable of retaining them, is less certain.

MRS BENNET

IMPORTANCE:

60%

Fact file:

○ Mrs Bennet is a very anxious, nervous and sensitive woman

○ She is always distressed about the entailment, so she wants all her daughters to get married so that the Bennet family will have some money and a place to live when Mr Bennet dies

○ She doesn't really like or understand Mr Bennet's sense of humour.

MR BENNET

IMPORTANCE:

50%

Fact file:

○ Mr Bennet is a sarcastic man who likes to joke

○ He is relaxed and doesn't worry much

○ He spends most of his time in his library reading

○ In the story, he realizes that he has been too relaxed as a parent, as the Bennet girls are not as educated or refined as they could have been.

MORE CHARACTERS ...

LYDIA

Appearance: Lydia is the tallest Bennet sister, even though she is the youngest. She is 'stout' and has 'a fine complexion'.

Fact file:

- Lydia loves to be around other people
- She jokes around a lot and doesn't take life too seriously
- She enjoys flirting with military men
- She gets her family into a lot of trouble when she runs off with Wickham.

KITTY

Also know as Catherine

Appearance: Kitty's appearance is not described by Austen, but we know she is prettier than Mary.

Fact file:

- Kitty spends a lot of her time with Lydia, following her around. She does not have a lot of independence
- Kitty is 17: the second youngest Bennet sister
- When Lydia gets married and leaves, Kitty starts to grow up and improve herself.

MARY

Appearance: Mary is 'the plain one in the family', meaning she is not pretty like her sisters.

Fact file:

- Mary enjoys reading books rather than spending time with people
- Even though she always reads, she isn't clever
- She loves impressing people
- At the end of the story, she starts to socialize more.

MR COLLINS

Also known as William Collins

Appearance: Mr Collins is 'tall' and 'heavy looking'.

Fact file:

- Mr Collins is a relative of the Bennet family. He will inherit the Bennets' estate when Mr Bennet dies
- The Bennets think he is ridiculous because he is too formal and polite, and he is not 'sensible'
- He talks a lot about Lady Catherine de Bourgh, a very rich lady who gave him his job and who impresses him very much.

MORE CHARACTERS . . .

CHARLOTTE

Full name: Charlotte Lucas

AKA: Charlotte Collins/ Mrs Collins

Appearance: Charlotte is about 27, 'very plain', meaning not very pretty.

Fact file:

- ✪ Charlotte is a close friend of the Bennets, especially Elizabeth
- ✪ She marries Mr Collins, probably because he has money, an inheritance and a house and connections.

CAROLINE

Full name: Caroline Bingley

Appearance: A 'fine' woman, her 'figure (is) elegant'. She has 'an air of decided fashion'.

Fact file:

- ✪ Caroline is Bingley's younger sister
- ✪ She tends to follow Bingley wherever he goes and look after his accommodation
- ✪ She spends a lot of time with her sister, Louisa. They both judge other people.

GEORGIANA

Full name: Georgiana Darcy

Appearance: 'tall', 'larger' than Elizabeth, but 'little more than sixteen'. She looks 'womanly' and 'graceful'.

Fact file:

- ✪ Georgiana is Darcy's younger sister
- ✪ Wickham tried to run away with her when she was fifteen for her money
- ✪ She is shy
- ✪ She is fond of Elizabeth.

MRS GARDINER

Appearance: She is younger than Mrs Bennet, and 'elegant'.

Fact file:

- ✪ Mrs Gardiner is Mrs Bennet's brother's wife, making her the Bennet girls' aunt
- ✪ The Bennet girls are all very fond of her
- ✪ She acts like a mother figure to Elizabeth, helping her think things through and talk about how she feels.

MORE CHARACTERS ...

LADY CATHERINE DE BOURGH

Appearance: She is 'a tall, large woman, with strongly marked features, which might once have been handsome'.

Fact file:

- Lady Catherine is a rich old lady who lives on an estate called Rosings
- She is Darcy's aunt and wants him to marry her daughter Anne
- She is used to people doing what she wants.

ANNE DE BOURGH

Appearance: She is 'thin and small' and 'sickly and cross'.

Fact file:

- Anne de Bourgh is Lady Catherine's daughter
- She always seems to look ill
- She doesn't talk much.

COLONEL FITZWILLIAM

Appearance: He is 'about thirty' and 'not handsome' but gentlemanly.

Fact file:

- Colonel Fitzwilliam is Darcy's cousin
- He is smart, polite, pleasant and friendly
- He seems to be attracted to Elizabeth, but she isn't interested.

MISS KING

Full name: Mary King

Appearance: Miss King is small and 'freckled'.

Fact file:

- Miss king is described as 'good', 'agreeable' and 'pleasant'
- She has recently become rich
- Wickham is very interested in her as soon as she gets her money.

What is a Theme?

A theme is an **idea** that comes up **again** and **again**.

The author will put themes in a book because they want the reader to think about certain things.

Themes carry **messages** and help to create an **effect** on the reader.

Here are some of the themes in *Pride and Prejudice*:

Marriage

Reputation

Love

Class

Use the following pages to help you decide which themes link to each other, and see if you can think of any more.

Remember: You can talk about themes in any exam question.

THEME:
Class

Class, means the group in society that a person is seen to belong to, based on their **wealth, influence, family**, job and other factors. It used to be a way of telling how important someone was, with the highest class being the **richest**, and the lowest class being the **poorest**.

In *Pride and Prejudice*, class is something that **keeps characters apart**. There is a class difference between the Bennet family and the Bingley and Darcy/ de Bourgh family, with the Bennet family being **less wealthy and 'important'**. This means the Bennet sisters have problems pursuing love and marriage with upper-class men.

When Darcy proposes to Elizabeth for the first time, he says he is not happy about loving her because she is **not upper class**, like him. Darcy also advises Bingley **not to marry Jane** partly because of her class. Lady Catherine is also very determined for Elizabeth **not to marry** Darcy because she isn't of a high enough class.

Think about:

Why do the richer, upper-class characters care more about keeping classes separate than the middle-class characters?

Today, class is much less important. Why do you think this is?

Quotations about class

LOUISA

chapter 8

I have an excessive regard for Jane Bennet, she is really a very sweet girl and I wish with all my heart she were settled. But, with such a father and mother, and such low connections I am afraid there is no chance of it.

ELIZABETH

chapter 21

We are not rich enough, or grand enough for (Darcy and Caroline).

chapter 56

Is (Wickham), is the son of (Darcy's) late father' steward to be his brother? Are the shades of Pemberley to be thus polluted?

LADY CATHERINE

chapter 10

Darcy had never been so bewitched by any woman as he was by her. He really believed that were it not for the inferiority of her connections he would be in some danger

AUSTEN
(author and narrator)

chapter 13

Mrs Bennet ... says to (Mr Collins) with some asperity that they were very well able to keep a good cook, and that her daughters had nothing to do in the kitchen.

THEME: Marriage

Marriage and **love** are two clearly linked themes in *Pride and Prejudice*, however, they are definitely not the same. In *Pride and Prejudice*, you might notice that the characters get married quickly, and although we read a lot about marriage, we don't read a lot about people falling in love.

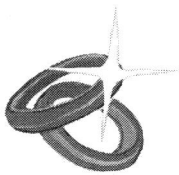

In *Pride and Prejudice* – and in English middle- and upper-class culture in the 18th century – marriage was not about getting together with someone you loved and spending a happy life together. Instead, it was often about **money**.

Think about:

Why is it so important that Wickham marries Lydia?

What would happen to the Bennet family if none of the girls got married?

Why does Lady Catherine want Darcy to marry her daughter Anne?

Quotations about marriage

CHARLOTTE

Happiness in marriage is entirely a matter of chance.

chapter 6

MRS BENNET

chapter 13

Things are settled so oddly.

(the entail) is a grievous affair to my poor girls.

chapter 13

chapter 47

Wickham will never marry a woman without some money.

ELIZABETH

WICKHAM

chapter 16

(Lady Catherine's) daughter ... will have a very large fortune, and it is believed that she and her cousin will unite the two estates.

THEME: Love

Love is a major theme in *Pride and Prejudice*, as the story follows Elizabeth and Darcy's journey to love and romance.

Elizabeth and Darcy's eventual love for each other is the major direction of the story, and Austen makes sure that the reader knows their love is true and genuine by having their love overcome all sorts of problems.

Elizabeth and Darcy end up together despite disliking each other at first, misunderstanding one another, coming from different backgrounds and the disapproval from their own families.

We could say the same about Jane and Bingley. Another couple who truly love each other, they end up together despite a big problem that could have stopped them – Darcy trying to keep them apart.

In the end, love ends up being more powerful and important than all of the problems that step in the way of these two couples. In writing this, Austen could be suggesting to the reader that love is far more important than class, background and other peoples' opinions.

Think about:

Which couples are truly in love?

Why is love less important than money to some characters?

How quickly does Elizabeth fall in love?

Quotations about love

CHARLOTTE

There are very few of us who have heart enough to be really in love without encouragement.

chapter 6

I am not a romantic you know. I ask only a comfortable home.

Chapter 22

DARCY

chapter 34

In vain I have struggled. It will not do. My feelings will not be repressed. You must allow me to tell you how ardently I admire and love you.

chapter 50

(Elizabeth) began now to comprehend that (Darcy) was exactly the man, who, in disposition and talents would most suit her.

AUSTEN (author and narrator)

chapter 59

I do like (Darcy) ... I love him. Indeed he has no improper pride. He is perfectly amiable. You do not know what he really is.

ELIZABETH

THEME:
Reputation

In middle- and upper-class English society in the late 18th and 19th century, it was extremely important to be **respected** by those around you, to appear to be a **good** and **very polite** person, and to act and appear **normal**. These were like rules people had to follow. If a person did not follow these **rules**, there could be consequences: they could lose friends, family members might stop talking to them or inviting them to social events. These things could even mean losing out on jobs or money!

Think about:

Does having a good reputation mean you are a good person?

Which characters care a lot about reputation? Which characters don't?

Quotations about reputation

LADY CATHERINE

I am no stranger to the particulars of your youngest sister's infamous elopement. I know it all; that the young man's marrying her was a patched-up business, at the expense of your father and uncles. And is such a girl to be my nephew's sister? Is her husband the son of his late father's steward, to be his brother? ... Are the shades of Pemberley to be thus polluted?

chapter 56

MARY

Loss of virtue in a female is irretrievable; that one false step involves her in endless ruin; that her reputation is no less brittle than it is beautiful.

chapter 47

chapter 46

this false step in one daughter will be injurious to fortunes of all the others: for who ... will connect themselves with such a family?

MR. COLLINS

chapter 46

Lydia – the humiliation, the misery she was bringing on them all, soon swallowed up every private care.

AUSTEN

(author and narrator)

What is Pride?

> The title *Pride and Prejudice* refers to the way that Elizabeth and Darcy act toward each other. It it important to know what the words 'pride' and 'prejudice' mean, and how the words are used in the book.

We might think that 'pride' is supposed to be something good – for example, if you take 'pride' in yourself or in your work, it means you care a lot about it and make it as good as possible.

However, pride can also be seen as a bad thing in a person. Especially in the book, the word 'pride' is often used negatively, especially when Elizabeth talks about Darcy. When she talks about Darcy's pride, Elizabeth means that Darcy thinks he is **better than** others. Wickham also says that Darcy has a lot of pride, and that Darcy is so proud that he doesn't speak to people lower in class than him.

Austen also wants the reader to understand that Elizabeth has pride too. After all, Elizabeth decides that Darcy is no good after meeting him just the once, and ignores Caroline's warning about Wickham because she doesn't like her.

Quotations about pride

WICKHAM

chapter 16

(Pride) has often led (Darcy) to be liberal and generous ... family pride, and *filial* pride – for he is very proud of what his father was – have done this.

chapter 16

Almost all (Darcy's) actions may be traced to pride; and pride had often been his best friend.

DARCY

Yes, vanity is a weakness indeed. But pride – where there is real superiority of mind, pride will be always under good regulation.

chapter 11

ELIZABETH

How despicably I have acted! I, who have prided myself on discernment! ... how humiliating is this discovery!

chapter 36

What is Prejudice?

The title *Pride and Prejudice* refers to the way that Elizabeth and Darcy act toward each other. It it important to know what the words 'pride' and 'prejudice' mean, and how the words are used in the book.

'Prejudice' is a word that literally means 'pre-judge': to judge someone before really knowing them. In the story, we see prejudice when characters (particularly Elizabeth) form an opinion of somebody else without getting to know that person first. Elizabeth does this with Darcy – she makes up her mind about him after meeting him just the once, thinking he is proud and not nice. Darcy notices Elizabeth's prejudice, and says that her fault is "wilfully to misunderstand everybody" in chapter 11.

Elizabeth does the same with Wickham – she makes up her mind quickly that he is a good man without really knowing him. This means that later in the story she is embarrassed about being wrong about the two men, and about acting unfairly towards Darcy because of her prejudice.

Darcy also shows prejudice in the story, which he eventually unlearns. He shows prejudice when he assumes none of the women at the Meryton Ball will 'tempt' him; when he proposes to Elizabeth whilst insulting her because of her class; and, when he splits up Bingley and Jane partly because of Jane's class.

Quotations about prejudice

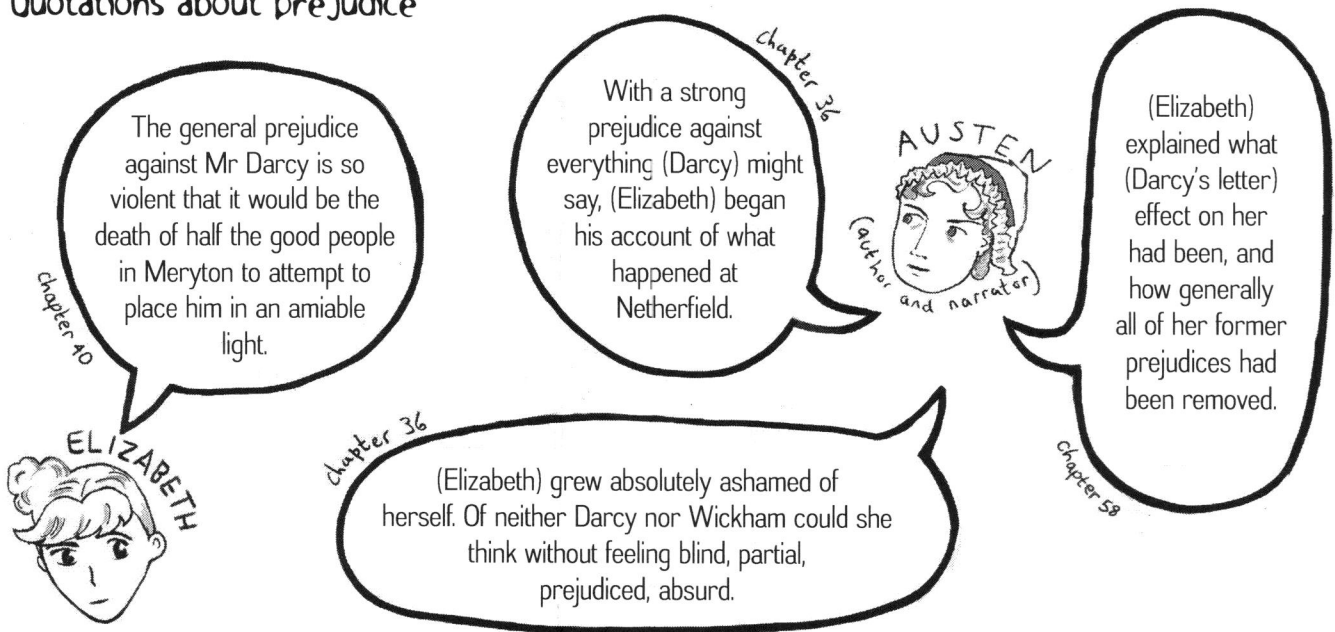

> The general prejudice against Mr Darcy is so violent that it would be the death of half the good people in Meryton to attempt to place him in an amiable light.

chapter 40

ELIZABETH

> With a strong prejudice against everything (Darcy) might say, (Elizabeth) began his account of what happened at Netherfield.

chapter 36

AUSTEN (author and narrator)

> (Elizabeth) explained what (Darcy's letter) effect on her had been, and how generally all of her former prejudices had been removed.

chapter 58

> (Elizabeth) grew absolutely ashamed of herself. Of neither Darcy nor Wickham could she think without feeling blind, partial, prejudiced, absurd.

chapter 36

An assembly

Pemberley

The Bennet Family

The Late Mr. Bennet

cousins

Mr Collins — Married — Charlotte

Mr. Bennet — married — Mrs Bennet

Mrs Phillips — Married — Mr. Phillips

Mr. Gardiner — Married — Mrs Gardiner

Lydia — Married — Wickham

Kitty

Mary

Elizabeth — Married — Darcy

Jane — Married — Bingley

Pride & Prejudice Map

The Lakes

DERBYSHIRE

Pemberley • Lambton

• Birmingham

• Cambridge

HERTFORDSHIRE

Longbourn

Meryton

• Netherfield

Rosings

★ London

• Hunsford •

Brighton

KENT

vocabulary

word	quote	meaning
accomplished	"(Georgiana) is a handsome girl, about fifteen or sixteen, and I understand, highly **accomplished**."	Having done and achieved a lot of good things.
acquaintance	"I think Mr Darcy improves on **acquaintance**."	Knowing someone; knowing what they are like.
amiable	"Indeed (Darcy) has no improper pride. He is perfectly **amiable**."	Likeable and pleasant.
clergyman	"I knew that Mr Wickham ought not to be a **clergyman**."	A man who works for the church, like a minister or priest.
condescension	"Lady Catherine, with great **condescension**, wished them a good journey."	(In the case of Pride and Prejudice) When an upper-class person lays aside any prejudices and willingly talks to a person of lower-class than them (especially Lady Catherine).

vocabulary

word	quote	meaning
entail/ entailed	"I can never be thankful, Mr Bennet, for anything about the **entail**." "Your father's estate is **entailed** to Mr Collins."	A type of inheritance which gives a family's estate to certain male relatives. This meant the head of the family could stay richer, as the estate was not divided up.
estate	"Mr Bennet's property consisted almost entirely in an **estate** of two thousand a year."	The property, land and money owned by a person or family.
imprudent	"I am afraid (Wickham) has been very **imprudent**, and has deserved to lose Darcy's regard."	Doing things without thinking them through first; making poor decisions.
militia	"(Kitty and Lydia) were well supplied both with news and happiness by the recent arrival of a **militia** regiment in the neighbourhood."	Part of the army that stays in their own country during a war (Home-guard).
parsonage	"Colonel Fitzwilliam's manners were very much admired at the **parsonage**."	A house next to and owned by the church for a member of the church to live in (like Mr Collins).
scandalous	"Darcy's behaviour to myself has been **scandalous**."	Behaviour so bad that people would gossip about it.

Who is being described?

Draw lines to match the description to the person.

"Whatever she said was spoken in so authoritative a tone, as marked her self-importance."

LADY CATHERINE

"There is something a little stately in him, to be sure ... but it is confined to his air, and is not unbecoming ... though some people may call him proud, I have seen nothing of it."

WICKHAM

"an amiable, intelligent, elegant woman"

MRS GARDINER

"as false and disagreeable as he is insulting"

CAROLINE

"she is not such a simpleton ... and she is the more anxious to get Miss Darcy for her brother".

ELIZABETH

"she had a lively, playful disposition, which delighted in anything ridiculous."

DARCY

What were they really thinking?

Here are some moments from *Pride and Prejudice* with thought bubbles added above some of the characters' heads. Write inside the bubble what you think the characters are really thinking in that moment.

What is Darcy thinking when Bingley tries to get him to dance at the public assembly. (Chapter 3)?

What are Darcy and Elizabeth thinking when Darcy is watching Elizabeth at the Lucas Lodge assembly. (Chapter 6)?

What were they really thinking?

Here are some moments from *Pride and Prejudice* with thought bubbles added above some of the characters' heads. Write inside the bubble what you think the characters are really thinking in that moment.

What is Darcy thinking when Caroline keeps trying to distract him from writing a letter to Georgiana. (Chapter 10)?

You write so quickly. How's that pen? Shall I mend it for you?

What are Darcy and Wickham thinking when they meet unexpectedly in Meryton, with the Bennet girls there too. (Chapter 15)?

Oh ... hello ...

This seems awkward.

What were they really thinking?

Here are some moments from *Pride and Prejudice* with thought bubbles added above some of the characters' heads. Write inside the bubble what you think the characters are really thinking in that moment.

What was Elizabeth thinking when Mr Collins proposed to her (Chapter 19)?

What was Elizabeth thinking when Colonel Fitzwilliam revealed that Darcy felt proud and happy about stopping Bingley from marrying Jane (Chapter 33)?

Who said it ?

Draw lines to match the speech to the person.

"I certainly have not the talent which some people possess ... of conversing easily with those I have never seen before. I cannot catch their tone of conversation, or appear interested in their concerns, as I often see done."

ELIZABETH

"Happiness in marriage is entirely a matter of chance."

DARCY

"I have courted prepossession and ignorance, and driven reason away, where either were concerned. Till this moment I never knew myself."

LADY CATHERINE

"Perhaps I do (dislike arguments). Arguments are too much like disputes. If you and Miss Bennet will defer yours till I am out of the room, I shall be very thankful ...."

CHARLOTTE

"My character has ever been celebrated for its sincerity and frankness."

MRS BENNET

"Nobody can tell what I suffer! – But it is always so. Those who do not complain are never pitied."

BINGLEY

Match the couples

Draw lines to match up who the married couples are at the end of the story.

WICKHAM

MR. COLLINS

BINGLEY

DARCY

CHARLOTTE

JANE

LYDIA

ELIZABETH

♡ _____ and _____

♡ _____ and _____

♡ _____ and _____

♡ _____ and _____

How would you feel if ...

Your best friend had the right to kick you out of your home? (It happens to Elizabeth, chapter 22+.)

A rich, attractive person said mean things about you, knowing you could hear them? (It happens to Elizabeth, chapter 3.)

Someone you really liked left town suddenly and didn't contact you? (It happens to Jane, chapter 21.)

Someone you liked believed false rumours about you, and rejected you because of them? (It happens to Darcy, chapter 34.)

Because of something someone in your family did, your reputation risks being in ruins? (It happens to the Bennet family, chapter 46.)

A person that you thought was rude, arrogant and unkind turns out to be the complete opposite? (It happens to Elizabeth, chapter 35+.)

TRUMP CARDS

Elizabeth

Wealth . . . .
Good reputation . . . .
Pretty / Handsome . . . . .
Proud . . . .
Prejudiced . . . .

Darcy

Wealth . . . .
Good reputation . . . .
Pretty / Handsome . . . . .
Proud . . . .
Prejudiced . . . .

Jane

Wealth . . . .
Good reputation . . . .
Pretty / Handsome . . . . .
Proud . . . .
Prejudiced . . . .

Bingley

Wealth . . . .
Good reputation . . . .
Pretty / Handsome . . . . .
Proud . . . .
Prejudiced . . . .

Wickham

Wealth . . . .
Good reputation . . . .
Pretty / Handsome . . . . .
Proud . . . .
Prejudiced . . . .

Mr. Collins

Wealth . . . .
Good reputation . . . .
Pretty / Handsome . . . . .
Proud . . . .
Prejudiced . . . .

Find an important quote said by this character:

Find an important quote about this character:

List five adjectives to describe them:

They like …

Character:

Age:

Job:

They dislike …

How do they dress?

draw them here:

How much do I like this character? (circle)

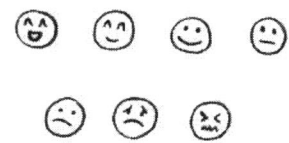

List three important things that happen to them in the story:

draw an item that links to them:

① _____

② _____

③ _____

Who are their friends?

QUOTE ANALYSIS

Chapter: Page: Said by:

Language techniques: Keywords:

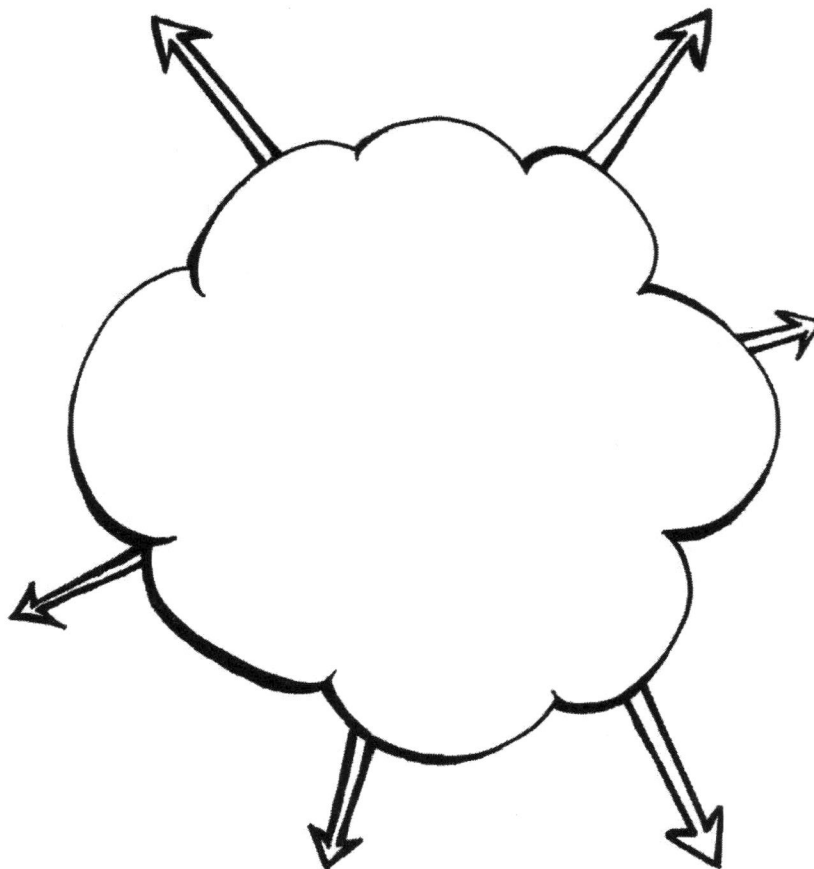

Most important
key word:

How does this
link to any of the
book's themes?

How does this link to
the context?

What other part of the
book does this link to?